The Graceful Healing
Workbook & Journal

A 12-Week Guided Journey for Emotional Wellness, Self-Healing, and Inner Renewal

ANA PARRA VIVAS

Copyright © 2026 Ana Parra Vivas

All rights reserved. No part of this publication may be reproduced, distributed, or transmitted in any form or by any means, including photocopying, recording, or other electronic or mechanical methods, without the prior written permission of the author, except in the case of brief quotations embodied in critical reviews and certain other noncommercial uses permitted by copyright law. **This work may not be used to train, fine-tune, or improve artificial intelligence or machine-learning systems, including any text and data mining, without the author's prior written consent.** For permission requests, email the author with "Attention: Permissions Coordinator" in the subject line at ana@anaparravivas.com

Disclaimer: This book is intended to offer information and inspiration to readers. It is provided with the understanding that the author is not engaged in rendering psychological, legal, or any other professional services. The views expressed in each article are solely those of the author. As a reader, you are responsible for your own decisions, actions, and outcomes.

ISBN: 979-8-9916340-2-1 (Paperback)
　　　979-8-9916340-3-8 (Hardcover)

Editor: Wildflower Books
Layout Artist: Praise Saflor

First printing edition 2026

WWW.ANAPARRAVIVAS.COM

Table of Contents

Introduction 5
How to Use This Workbook & Journal 7
A Note on Language 8
A Gentle Invitation 10

Month 1: Mental Alignment and Self-Discovery 11

Week 1: My Mind Is My Medicine 12
Week 2: Are You Blocking Your Own Success? 18
Week 3: From Fear to Faith 24
Week 4: Overcoming the Fear of Change 30

Month 2: Energy, Intuition, and Inspired Action 37

Week 5: What Are You Sending Out to the Universe? 38
Week 6: The Law of Receiving 44
Week 7: Managing Your Inner World to Overcome Challenges .. 50
Week 8: A Blueprint for Reaching Your Goals 56

Month 3: Manifestation, Abundance, and Trust 62

Week 9: The Time It Takes for Dreams to Manifest 63
Week 10: How to Attract Prosperity and Health 69
Week 11: Be Confident, Even with an Empty Bank Account 75
Week 12: Be the Source of Abundance 82

Closing Reflection: You Did It 88
Final Reflection Questions 89
Closing Affirmation 92
A Note from Ana 93
I'd Love to Hear from You! 94
Your Journey Doesn't End Here 95
Additional Resources to Support Your Journey 97
About the Author 100

DEDICATION

To my husband, Ivan, for your steady love and faithful support.

Introduction

Welcome to The Graceful Healing Workbook & Journal

I don't know if you're just starting on this path or if you've been reading self-help books for years. But whatever brought you here, trust that you are exactly where you need to be.

One thing life has shown me is this: we can collect knowledge forever, but true change only happens when we practice. That's why I created this journal the way I did. It's not just for reading. It's for doing. For experiencing. For remembering what you already know deep inside.

Many years ago, I started writing weekly emails to my readers — short messages I called Manifest Mondays. They were inspired by a simple question. *What if we could stop dreading Mondays and begin seeing them as a sacred start?* A fresh chance to align with what we want, who we are, and how we want to show up in the world.

Those letters were often born from something I was learning or reflecting on in real time. I'm a teacher, yes, but I'm also a student. I'm still growing. So I'd write about what I noticed in my life, with my clients, in the world, or even on social media. That's why people said they felt these emails were "perfectly timed." They came from presence. That's the energy this journal carries too.

This journal is designed to help you *practice* the principles — not just think about them. Through thoughtful questions and weekly reflections, you'll move from knowing to *understanding*. Because when you start asking questions, your mind starts answering. The wisdom is already inside you.

And if a question doesn't resonate right away, that's okay. Come back to it later. You may not yet be in tune with the vibration of that question, and that's not a flaw; it's just timing.

Once, while studying with Bob Proctor, I told him I didn't understand a book he had recommended. He paused and said, "Put it down. Come back in a few months. You're not in tune with its vibration yet." He was right. When I returned to the book after more inner work, it suddenly made sense.

So take your time with this journal. Don't rush. Let the questions stir you. Let your thoughts breathe on paper.

Journaling is a powerful spiritual practice. When we write things down, we don't just clarify our thoughts. We signal to the Divine Spirit that we're ready. Ready to receive more. Ready to expand.

The Graceful Healing Workbook & Journal can be used on its own, but if you'd like to go deeper, I highly recommend my book *I Trust My Inner Voice*. It includes detailed explanations and visual guides to many of the concepts referenced here. You don't have to read it to benefit from this journal, but if you feel called, it can help deepen your understanding.

Welcome to the journey. I'm honored to walk alongside you.

With love,
Ana

How to Use This Workbook & Journal

This is a 12-week guided journey, meant to help you shift the way you think so you can shift the way you live.

Each week, you'll find:

- ★ A short message to realign your thoughts with truth
- ★ Six deep questions to open your awareness and shift old patterns
- ★ An affirmation to anchor new beliefs
- ★ A sacred space for reflection and healing

You are not here to rush.

You are here to remember.

Go at your own pace. Let the words meet you where you are. Some women move through one week at a time. Others sit with the same lesson for several days. There's no wrong way, only your way.

If something stirs, stay with it. If something feels new, trust it.

You may return to this journal again and again. Your answers will evolve as *you* do.

Let this be your quiet place to listen. To feel. To ask better questions.
Let it become a practice, a daily return to your Inner Voice and to Divine Spirit.

Healing begins when we choose to see differently.

That choice starts here.

A Note on Language

In this journal, you'll often see me refer to **Infinite Intelligence**, **Divine Spirit**, and your **Inner Voice**.

These are not abstract concepts to me. They're the living forces that guide, heal, and hold us every day.

- **Infinite Intelligence** is the universal, all-knowing source of wisdom, ideas, and creative power.

  Napoleon Hill described it as the **higher force that knows all truths**, that guides us through intuition and responds when we align our thoughts with faith, clarity, and purpose. It's not limited to any one belief system.

  Infinite Intelligence is the invisible force that helps turn thoughts into things when we trust it, connect with it, and act in harmony with it.

- **Divine Spirit** is another word for the **Holy Spirit** or **Life Force**, the sacred energy that flows through all living things. It's the presence of God within us and around us.

  Some experience it as light, sound, peace, or a deep inner knowing. It's the part of God we can feel, the voice that guides us, the energy that gives us life.

  When we connect with **Divine Spirit**, we align with love, truth, and the higher plan for our lives.

- Your **Inner Voice** is how **Infinite Intelligence** and **Divine Spirit** often speak to you, through nudges, knowing, and quiet reminders that you are safe, guided, and loved. This is represented by nudges, intuition, inspiration, instinct, feeling, gut reaction, sixth sense, perception, or reasoning.

- **Conscious Mind:** The mind can be thought of as divided in two parts: the conscious mind and the subconscious mind. The conscious mind, the thinking mind, has thoughts and knowledge. It is the intellectual mind.

When you went to school, you kept the ideas and knowledge you learned in the conscious mind. For a deeper explanation of these terms, including illustrations and examples, see my book *I Trust My Inner Voice* by Ana Parra Vivas.

- **Subconscious Mind**: This is home to your paradigm. The ideas that have been impressed through repetition by the conscious mind are in your subconscious mind. The subconscious mind does not have the ability to reject; it accepts everything that the conscious mind sends it.

- **Paradigm**: This is a collection of beliefs and concepts based on assumptions you make from the information you receive from the outside world. For example, your political ideology, how you see other races, your outlook on finances and money, and even your opinion of yourself (self-worth). These are all part of your paradigm, your own view of the world.

- **Mantras**: Since words are representations of the sound of God, there are special sounds or words that put us in alignment with it. When we say special mantras, we are putting ourselves in the same frequency with light and sound.

- **HU, a sacred sound**: **HU** (pronounced *Huuuuuuuuu*, like "hue" with the "u" extended softly) is a sacred mantra, an ancient name for God. With eyes open or closed, take a few deep breaths to relax. Then begin to sing **HU** in a long, drawn-out sound. **HU-U-U-U**. Take another breath, and sing **HU** again. Continue for up to twenty minutes. Sing **HU** with a feeling of love, and it will gradually open your heart to Divine Love.
  For thousands of years, people from many spiritual paths have used **HU** as a way to attune to the presence of the Divine.

  It can be sung aloud or silently as a prayer, a meditation, or simply a way to reconnect with peace and clarity. Millions of people around the world have experienced the joy, love, and calm that comes from chanting **HU**. You can use it anytime, especially when you want to feel supported, centered, or connected to something greater.

Throughout this journal, I invite you to use the words that feel right to you. The truth is the same: you are never alone.

A Gentle Invitation

If you'd like to deepen your connection with the Divine as you move through this journal, you're welcome to include a simple spiritual practice like the **HU** mantra. It's not required, but it can be a powerful companion for those who feel called to explore it.

To learn how to use **HU** in your practice and explore other gentle resources for healing and inner alignment, visit: **www.anaparravivas.com/graceful-healing**

This is your journey.
Trust your own rhythm.
Trust your Inner Voice.

MONTH 1:

Mental Alignment and Self-Discovery

Welcome to the first month of your *The Graceful Healing Workbook & Journal* journey.

These first four weeks are designed to help you reconnect with yourself gently and intentionally. You'll begin by tuning into your thoughts, noticing what's been guiding your choices, and realigning your self-image with the life you truly want to create.

This is not about doing more. It's about becoming more aware of the beliefs, emotions, and patterns that shape your reality.

You may sometimes feel like you're not doing enough. But please hear this: **you're doing more than most people will ever dare to do.** You are choosing to grow, to feel, to reflect, and that's real progress. That's courageous.

This month, you'll begin to:
- Understand how your mind influences your emotions, health, and results
- Recognize the quiet thoughts that may be blocking your success
- Shift from fear into faith
- Reconnect with the wisdom that already lives within you

Take it one week at a time. Give yourself permission to slow down, to feel, and to trust the process. You're not starting from scratch. You're coming back to your center.

Week 1: My Mind Is My Medicine

Your thoughts shape your energy, health, and future.
Awareness is your first tool for transformation.

This Week's Message

You've probably heard this before — that you can heal yourself using only your mind.

I used to wonder, *How does that actually work?* It sounded magical but distant. Like something others could do, but not me.

Now I know: it's not magic; it's alignment. When I'm calm, centered, and connected to my inner guidance, answers always come. Sometimes, they arrive as a whisper. Other times, they appear as a sense of clarity in the middle of a walk or a quiet nudge to make a change. It feels like I'm being guided by something deeper than my thoughts, something wise and gentle.

That's my subconscious mind in tune with Infinite Intelligence. And it's available to all of us.

Here's how I strengthen that connection:

- **Meditation**: I keep it simple. I close my eyes, imagine a soft blue light around me, chant a mantra, or breathe slowly — in for three, hold for two, out for four.

- **Visualization**: I ask myself, *If my dream is fulfilled, how would I feel?* I let that feeling wash over me.

- **Stillness**: I listen. I trust the answer will come, and it always does.

The more I practice, the more I trust. And the more I trust, the more peaceful and powerful I feel.

If things aren't going how you expected right now, it's okay. This might be your invitation to reconnect, to pause and receive new direction.

You don't have to figure it all out. You just have to listen.

Pause & Reflect

When have I felt deeply guided or supported, even if I didn't understand why at the time?

_____
_____
_____
_____
_____
_____
_____
_____
_____
_____

What practices help me quiet my mind and feel more peaceful?

_____
_____
_____
_____
_____
_____
_____
_____
_____
_____

Pause & Reflect

Do I believe that my mind can influence my body and emotions? Why or why not?

_____
_____
_____
_____
_____
_____
_____
_____
_____
_____

What small ritual could I try this week to strengthen my connection to inner guidance?

_____
_____
_____
_____
_____
_____
_____
_____

Pause & Reflect

How would it feel to trust that answers are already on their way?

_____
_____
_____
_____
_____
_____
_____
_____
_____

What would it feel like to fully trust that I already have access to the answers I need?

_____
_____
_____
_____
_____
_____
_____
_____

Anchor This Truth

"My mind is calm, clear, and connected to the wisdom I need."

Write your own version of this affirmation, or describe what it brings up for you.

_____
_____
_____
_____
_____
_____
_____
_____
_____
_____
_____
_____
_____
_____
_____
_____
_____
_____
_____
_____
_____
_____
_____
_____

Inner Voice Journal

Use this space to reflect on anything that came up for you during this week's message or the weekly questions.

You may want to return to one or two of the questions and explore them more deeply here. Let your writing flow freely. There's no right or wrong way to do this.

You can also journal about:
- A moment this week when you felt in tune — or out of tune
- What your body or intuition is trying to tell you
- A situation where you could apply the principle *"My mind is my medicine"*

Let your Inner Voice speak freely.

Week 2: Are You Blocking Your Own Success?

Identify the invisible habits and beliefs that quietly sabotage your goals, and learn how to let them go.

This Week's Message

I didn't always realize it, but for a long time, I was the one standing in my own way.

It wasn't because I lacked potential. It was because I had a limited image of who I thought I was allowed to be.

Your **self-image** — the beliefs you hold about yourself — quietly shapes what you allow yourself to pursue, receive, and expect. This can open doors or keep them shut.

As I've continued to grow, I've learned to expand my self-image to match the life I want to create.

Here are some common self-blocking beliefs I've heard (and used myself):

"I'll believe it when I see it."
But real change starts when we flip this.
"I'll see it when I believe it."

Your mind is the gateway. When you believe something is possible for you — deeply, consistently — you begin to align with it, attract it, and become the version of you who already lives it.

Another block I've seen (and felt):

"I'm not ready."
But what if readiness isn't something you wait for?
What if it's something you decide?

When you trust your Inner Voice, you begin to see that even failure is part of the unfolding. You'll never feel fully ready. But with faith, practice, and self-trust, you'll know: **you're ready enough** to begin.

Pause & Reflect

What old belief or story might be blocking my success right now?

_____
_____
_____
_____
_____
_____
_____
_____
_____
_____

Do I tend to wait until I see it before I believe something is possible?

_____
_____
_____
_____
_____
_____
_____
_____
_____
_____

Pause & Reflect

What would it look like to believe in myself more deeply this week?

_____
_____
_____
_____
_____
_____
_____
_____
_____
_____

Where in my life am I telling myself, *"I'm not ready,"* and what if I am?

_____
_____
_____
_____
_____
_____
_____
_____

Pause & Reflect

How can I expand my self-image to match the life I truly want?

_____
_____
_____
_____
_____
_____
_____
_____
_____
_____

If I already believed I was worthy and ready, what decision or action would I take today?

_____
_____
_____
_____
_____
_____
_____
_____
_____

Anchor This Truth

"I'll see it when I believe it. I choose to believe in my worth, my readiness, and my future."

Write your own version of this affirmation, or reflect on how it feels for you today.

___
___
___
___
___
___
___
___
___
___
___
___
___
___
___
___
___
___
___
___
___
___
___
___
___
___
___

Inner Voice Journal

Use this space to reflect on what came up for you in the message and the weekly questions.

You may want to revisit a question that stirred something, or write freely about:
- A belief you're ready to release
- A part of your life where you're waiting to feel ready
- What shifted when you chose to believe instead of doubt

Let your Inner Voice speak freely.

Week 3: From Fear to Faith

A simple, powerful shift that moves you from anxiety into alignment with the version of you who already knows it's possible.

This Week's Message

"Faith and fear both demand you believe in something you cannot see. You choose."
— Bob Proctor

The first time I heard Bob say this, it stopped me in my tracks. Bob was my mentor, and his teachings continue to guide me. Especially this one.

Faith and fear are two sides of the same coin. According to the **Law of Polarity**, everything has an opposite. If there's darkness, there's light. If there's down, there's up. And if there's fear, there's faith.

So when we're caught in fear, we're simply tuned to one end of the spectrum. But we can shift. We can move toward faith.

Here's a simple three-step technique I use to move from fear to faith:

1. Identify the Fear

Fear often shows up as unwanted thoughts — worry, doubt, or imagining the worst. Notice it. Name it.

2. Ask Yourself: "Do I Want to Feel This?"

If the answer is no, then change the channel.

3. Choose Better Feelings

Shift your focus by asking:
- *What would I love?*
- *How would I feel if I already had it?*

When you focus on what you love and how you want to feel, you return to the vibration of **faith**. And in that vibration, you begin to manifest what you truly desire.

This takes practice, but it's worth it. You already have the power to choose.

Pause & Reflect

What fear has been showing up for me recently?

_____
_____
_____
_____
_____
_____
_____
_____
_____
_____

What thoughts or stories feed this fear?

_____
_____
_____
_____
_____
_____
_____
_____
_____
_____

Pause & Reflect

Pause and ask, *"Do I want to feel this?"* What's the answer?

_____
_____
_____
_____
_____
_____
_____
_____
_____
_____

What would I love to experience instead?

_____
_____
_____
_____
_____
_____
_____
_____
_____
_____

Pause & Reflect

How would it feel to fully trust that everything is working out for me?

_____
_____
_____
_____
_____
_____
_____
_____
_____

What small shift can I make this week to choose faith over fear?

_____
_____
_____
_____
_____
_____
_____
_____

Anchor This Truth

**"I release fear and return to faith.
I choose to focus on what I love and trust it's already mine."**

Write your own version of this affirmation, or reflect on how it feels in your body and mind.

Inner Voice Journal

Use this space to explore what came up for you in the message and the weekly questions.

You might write about:
- A moment you recognized fear and shifted it
- Something you would love to feel more of
- What faith looks like in your day-to-day life

Let your Inner Voice speak freely.

Week 4: Overcoming the Fear of Change

Why we resist transformation and how to stop fearing the unknown and start stepping into it with grace.

This Week's Message

Change is inevitable. Everything in life shifts, whether we move with it or resist it.

And yet, many of us stay stuck in situations we've outgrown because we're afraid of what comes next. I've seen it (and lived it). This might look like:

- Staying in a job that drains you because you're afraid there's nothing better
- Holding on to a relationship out of fear of being alone
- Silencing a dream because you're afraid to fail

Where does this fear come from?

Fear is a product of the thoughts in your mind. It's a mental process that is causing worry and doubt to arise within you. And since it's a mental process, you can train and use your mind to stop it and live a more satisfying life.

Here are the tools that have helped me (and many others) transform fear into courage.

Educate Yourself

Ignorance feeds fear. The more you understand, the less mysterious and overwhelming change becomes. Ask questions. Learn. Replace assumptions with facts.

Commit to Feeling Good

Gratitude is one of the most powerful emotional states we can enter. You can't feel fear and true gratitude at the same time. When fear creeps in, pause and focus on what you're thankful for. Let it shift your energy.

Imagine the Best Outcome Possible

Your mind already creates worst-case scenarios, so why not let it create the best-case alternative? Picture yourself on the other side of fear — successful, proud, peaceful. Let that vision guide you forward.

Pause & Reflect

What change in my life am I currently resisting and why?

_____
_____
_____
_____
_____
_____
_____
_____
_____
_____

What is the story I've been telling myself about what could go wrong?

_____
_____
_____
_____
_____
_____
_____
_____
_____
_____

Pause & Reflect

What facts or information could help me feel more confident about this change?

_____
_____
_____
_____
_____
_____
_____
_____
_____
_____

How can I use gratitude this week to calm my fear and raise my energy?

_____
_____
_____
_____
_____
_____
_____
_____
_____

Pause & Reflect

What would it look like to fully trust the next step?

_____
_____
_____
_____
_____
_____
_____
_____
_____
_____

If everything went beautifully, how would I feel on the other side of this change?

_____
_____
_____
_____
_____
_____
_____
_____

Anchor This Truth

*"I trust that change is here to help me grow.
I imagine the best, and I move forward with grace."*

Write your own version of this affirmation, or describe what it brings up for you.

_____
_____
_____
_____
_____
_____
_____
_____
_____
_____
_____
_____
_____
_____
_____
_____
_____
_____
_____
_____
_____
_____
_____

Inner Voice Journal

Use this space to explore what came up for you in the message and the weekly questions.

Write freely about:
- A change you're currently facing (or avoiding)
- A moment this week when you chose trust over fear
- A vision of yourself succeeding — what does it look and feel like?

Let your Inner Voice speak freely.

MONTH 2:

Energy, Intuition, and Inspired Action

Take a deep breath.

You've just completed one full month of inner alignment work, and that matters more than you know.

Over the past four weeks, you've begun shifting from old thoughts and fears into deeper awareness and trust. You've laid the foundation. Now it's time to tune your energy and move forward with intention.

This month, we'll focus on:

- The signals you're sending to the Universe

- The energy you're receiving in return

- The actions you're inspired to take from a place of clarity, not pressure

Remember: manifestation isn't about force. It's about alignment.
Let's continue, one aligned step at a time.

Week 5: What Are You Sending Out to the Universe?

*Your energy is always broadcasting.
Learn to send signals that reflect what you actually want to receive.*

This Week's Message

Every day, with every thought, emotion, and action, you're sending out a message to the Universe.

That message is your **attitude**, and it's magnetic.

Attitude is more than just mood. It's the vibration you carry into your relationships, your work, and your dreams. If you're constantly frustrated, anxious, or resentful, you might be unintentionally attracting more of the same. But when you shift into gratitude, curiosity, or joy — even for a few minutes — your entire field begins to change.

I know it's not easy to stay positive all day long. I'm a mom of two active kids, and some days start in chaos. But I've learned to switch gears quickly. I remind myself: *everything is for me*. Even the traffic. Even the challenge. Even the delay.

Here's what I suggest:

- **Decide what you want.** Clarity creates alignment.

- **Act like the person you want to become.** Embody her energy now.

- **Be grateful daily.** Gratitude magnetizes what you desire.

If you're not as happy, healthy, or abundant as you'd like to be, don't judge yourself. Just check the signal you're sending out. You have the power to reset at any moment. Your next manifestation begins with your next emotion.

Pause & Reflect

What energy have I been sending out recently in my thoughts, words, or actions?

_____
_____
_____
_____
_____
_____
_____
_____
_____
_____

Is that energy aligned with the life I say I want?

_____
_____
_____
_____
_____
_____
_____

Pause & Reflect

What would I love to attract more of?

_____
_____
_____
_____
_____
_____
_____
_____
_____
_____

How can I embody the version of me who already has that?

_____
_____
_____
_____
_____
_____
_____
_____
_____

Pause & Reflect

When I feel off, what helps me reset and shift into a better vibration?

_____
_____
_____
_____
_____
_____
_____
_____
_____

What's one attitude shift I can practice this week?

_____
_____
_____
_____
_____
_____
_____
_____

Anchor This Truth

"I am magnetic. I send out energy that matches the life I want to live."

Write your own version of this affirmation, or reflect on how it makes you feel.

_____
_____
_____
_____
_____
_____
_____
_____
_____
_____
_____
_____
_____
_____
_____
_____
_____
_____
_____
_____
_____
_____
_____
_____
_____

Inner Voice Journal

Use this space to explore what came up for you in the message and the weekly questions.

You might write about:
- A moment when your attitude shifted your day
- Something you're consciously sending out this week
- A new way you showed up as your future self

Let your Inner Voice speak freely.

Week 6: The Law of Receiving

*This often-forgotten law reminds us that receiving is an art,
one that begins with self-worth, openness, and trust.*

This Week's Message

The Law of Receiving is one of the most overlooked spiritual laws, but it's also one of the most powerful.

Many people are great at giving. They give their time, energy, support, love. But when it comes to **receiving**, they block the flow.

Here's what I've learned: receiving starts with **self-worth**.

If we don't believe we're worthy of love, support, success, or abundance, we'll deflect it, even when it's being offered freely. We'll downplay compliments, reject help, or question people's intentions. Not because we're ungrateful but because we've been conditioned to believe we don't deserve to receive.

The Law of Receiving is deeply connected to **gratitude** and **openness**.

To practice it:

- Allow yourself to be successful.

- Give yourself love, rest, and compassion.

- Offer compliments and kindness freely, without expecting anything back.

- Receive with grace — a smile, a gift, a compliment, a helping hand.

When someone compliments you, say, *"Thank you for noticing."*
When someone offers help, say, *"Yes, thank you."*
No guilt. No resistance. Just *receive*.

You are worthy of all the good that wants to find you.
When you receive with joy, you honor the giver and the Universe.

Pause & Reflect

How comfortable am I with receiving — compliments, support, help, or gifts?

_____
_____
_____
_____
_____
_____
_____
_____
_____
_____

Do I ever deflect kindness because I feel unworthy or suspicious of it?

_____
_____
_____
_____
_____
_____
_____
_____

Pause & Reflect

How does my ability to receive reflect my relationship with self-worth?

_____
_____
_____
_____
_____
_____
_____
_____
_____
_____

What would it look like to welcome more abundance and support into my life this week?

_____
_____
_____
_____
_____
_____
_____
_____

Pause & Reflect

What is one compliment, offer, or gift I could receive with openness?

_____
_____
_____
_____
_____
_____
_____
_____
_____
_____
_____

What can I give freely this week — love, appreciation, attention — without expecting anything in return?

_____
_____
_____
_____
_____
_____
_____
_____
_____
_____

Anchor This Truth

"I am open to receive. I am worthy of love, support, and abundance in every form."

Write your own version of this affirmation, or describe what it brings up for you.

_____
_____
_____
_____
_____
_____
_____
_____
_____
_____
_____
_____
_____
_____
_____
_____
_____
_____
_____
_____
_____
_____
_____
_____
_____

Inner Voice Journal

Use this space to reflect on your experience with the **Law of Receiving** and this week's questions.

Consider journaling about:
- A moment when you received something and how you responded
- A shift in your ability to say yes without guilt
- A time you gave something freely, from love, not expectation

Let your Inner Voice speak freely.

Week 7: Managing Your Inner World to Overcome Challenges

Three grounding tools to navigate emotional storms and stay anchored in your power.

This Week's Message

We can't always control what happens around us, but we can influence how we respond within ourselves.

Your **inner world** — your thoughts, emotions, and beliefs — is the lens through which you experience everything. When it's calm, focused, and nurtured, even life's challenges become easier to handle. But when it's cluttered with fear, self-judgment, or pressure, everything feels harder than it needs to be.

Here are the gentle tools I return to whenever life feels overwhelming.

Switch from Negative to Positive

When something throws you off — a conversation, a delay, a disappointment — pause and ask, *"What would I love?"* This question helps shift your energy and focus. It brings you back to your vision instead of keeping you stuck in the problem.

Visit Your Quiet Room

Inspired by Dr. Maxwell Maltz's work in *Psycho-Cybernetics*, this practice helps you reset throughout the day. Imagine a beautiful, calming space — a room created in your mind with soft colors, a comfy chair, and a peaceful view. Between tasks or in stressful moments, close your eyes, breathe deeply, and spend three minutes there. It's a mini vacation for your nervous system.

Practice Self-Compassion

Say to yourself, *"I forgive myself for not being perfect."* Let go of the pressure to get it all right. You're doing more than enough. You are learning, expanding, and showing up, and that's more than most people ever do.

Managing your inner world isn't about control. It's about **gentle awareness** and **daily practice.**

Pause & Reflect

What recent situation challenged my peace, and how did I respond?

_____
_____
_____
_____
_____
_____
_____
_____
_____
_____

What thoughts or patterns tend to pull me out of alignment?

_____
_____
_____
_____
_____
_____
_____
_____

Pause & Reflect

How might the question *"What would I love?"* help me shift my focus this week?

_____
_____
_____
_____
_____
_____
_____
_____
_____
_____

What does my ideal quiet room look and feel like? When could I visit it?

_____
_____
_____
_____
_____
_____
_____
_____
_____

Pause & Reflect

How kind am I being to myself lately? Where can I offer more grace?

_____
_____
_____
_____
_____
_____
_____
_____
_____
_____

What small practice could help me stay more centered when life gets noisy?

_____
_____
_____
_____
_____
_____
_____
_____
_____
_____

Anchor This Truth

"I care for my inner world with gentleness and awareness. Peace is always available within me."

Write your own version of this affirmation, or reflect on how it makes you feel.

_____
_____
_____
_____
_____
_____
_____
_____
_____
_____
_____
_____
_____
_____
_____
_____
_____
_____
_____
_____
_____
_____
_____
_____
_____

Inner Voice Journal

Use this space to explore what came up for you in this week's message and questions.

You might write about:
- A moment when you shifted from stress to calm
- What your inner quiet room feels like
- What changed when you responded with self-compassion

Let your Inner Voice speak freely.

Week 8: A Blueprint for Reaching Your Goals

A soulful four-step method to move from vision to results without burnout or doubt.

This Week's Message

Why are goals so important?

Because when you pursue the *right* goals — goals that stretch you and excite you — you grow. You become more aware, more focused, more alive. And you become someone who can help and inspire others too.

But too often, we aim small. We play it safe. We set goals based on where we are, not where we could go.

Here's a **soulful four-step blueprint** I use to create goals that feel aligned, expansive, and doable — without burnout or self-doubt.

Step 1: Decide Where You're Going

Dream bigger than you've ever allowed yourself to. Don't base your vision on what you've already done. Create from faith, not history. Use your imagination. Align with Divine Spirit. Think: *What would I truly love?*

Step 2: Get Honest About Where You Are Now

Be loving but honest. What's working? What needs to shift? What knowledge, mindset, or habits must evolve?

Step 3: Pay the Price

There's always a cost. Maybe it's releasing an old identity, waking up earlier, or letting go of distractions. Ask yourself: *Am I willing to pay the price to bring this vision into form?*

Step 4: Commit

Make the decision to show up daily. Even when it's hard. Especially when it's hard. Your commitment sends a message to the Universe: *I'm ready.*

Pause & Reflect

What's one BIG goal I would love to achieve, even if it feels out of reach right now?

_____
_____
_____
_____
_____
_____
_____
_____
_____
_____

What limiting thoughts or beliefs might be keeping me stuck in small goals?

_____
_____
_____
_____
_____
_____
_____
_____

Pause & Reflect

Where am I now — emotionally, mentally, spiritually — in relation to that goal?

_____
_____
_____
_____
_____
_____
_____
_____
_____
_____

What habits or changes would help me close the gap between where I am and where I want to be?

_____
_____
_____
_____
_____
_____
_____
_____
_____

Pause & Reflect

Am I truly willing to pay the price? If not, what's holding me back?

_____
_____
_____
_____
_____
_____
_____
_____
_____
_____

What will committing to this goal look like for me this week?

_____
_____
_____
_____
_____
_____
_____
_____
_____

Anchor This Truth

**"I am willing, I am capable, and I am committed.
My vision is worthy of my energy and action."**

Write your own version of this affirmation, or reflect on what it stirs in you.

Inner Voice Journal

Use this space to explore your relationship with goals and what this week's message brought up for you.

You might write about:
- A big vision you're ready to claim
- An honest look at your current reality
- A new commitment or small decision you made this week

Let your Inner Voice speak freely.

MONTH 3:

Manifestation, Abundance, and Trust

You've made it to month three, and whether it feels like it or not, you've already shifted so much.

Over the past eight weeks, you've shown up for yourself with intention. You've listened inward, released old patterns, and begun to realign with the version of you that lives with clarity and calm.

In this final month, we move into the heart of manifestation.

This is where you'll begin to:
- Deepen your trust in divine timing
- Raise your vibration through gratitude and joy
- Become more open to receiving
- Step fully into the identity of someone who **already lives in abundance**

You don't need to force or chase anything. You're here to **receive, align**, and **allow**.

Let this month be a celebration of all the seeds you've planted and a quiet trust that what you desire is already finding its way to you.

You are magnetic.
You are ready.
Let's begin.

Week 9: The Time It Takes for Dreams to Manifest

*Timing is divine. Learn how to stay faithful
while your desires are taking root behind the scenes.*

This Week's Message

"Nothing great is created suddenly, any more than a bunch of grapes or a fig.
If you tell me that you desire a fig, I answer you that there must be time.
Let it first blossom, then bear fruit, then ripen."
— Epictetus, Greek Stoic Philosopher (50–135 AD)

We live in a fast-paced world, but true creation takes time.

I've spoken with so many women who feel anxious because their goals aren't manifesting fast enough. They want to lose twenty pounds in a month. They want the job or the breakthrough *now*. And when it doesn't happen quickly, doubt creeps in.

But here's the truth: **when you expect failure, you attract it.**

Many people don't realize they're carrying silent disbelief. They try new things, but deep down, they expect to be disappointed — again. And that expectation becomes their experience.

If that's been your pattern, you're not alone. But you can shift it.

Here's what has helped me:

- **Feel it as if it's already here.** Imagine yourself *living* the outcome you desire. Not someday. *Now*. See it. Feel it. Become it.

- **Trust Infinite Intelligence.** Know that you are worthy of success and that the timing will be perfect. The goal is not just coming; it's being prepared for you.

- **Nourish your belief.** Read, listen, and study to strengthen your faith, not just in the goal but in yourself.

Remember, it takes nine months to birth a baby. Manifesting your dream may take time, but when it comes, it will be *exactly right*.

Pause & Reflect

What goal or desire have I felt impatient about?

_____
_____
_____
_____
_____
_____
_____
_____
_____
_____

What silent doubts or fears might be affecting my energy or expectations?

_____
_____
_____
_____
_____
_____
_____
_____
_____
_____

Pause & Reflect

How can I start *feeling* as if my goal is already here?

_____
_____
_____
_____
_____
_____
_____
_____
_____
_____

What practices help me strengthen my trust in divine timing?

_____
_____
_____
_____
_____
_____
_____
_____

Pause & Reflect

How might my journey be preparing me in ways I can't yet see?

_____
_____
_____
_____
_____
_____
_____
_____
_____
_____

What would change if I believed success was already mine?

_____
_____
_____
_____
_____
_____
_____
_____
_____
_____

Anchor This Truth

"I trust the timing of my dreams. What I desire is already mine, and I am aligning with it more each day."

Write your own version of this affirmation, or reflect on what it awakens in you.

_____
_____
_____
_____
_____
_____
_____
_____
_____
_____
_____
_____
_____
_____
_____
_____
_____
_____
_____
_____
_____
_____

Inner Voice Journal

Use this space to reflect on your relationship with time, patience, and belief.

You might write about:
- A desire you're still waiting on
- A moment when divine timing showed up perfectly in the past
- What you're learning while you wait

Let your Inner Voice speak freely.

Week 10: How to Attract Prosperity and Health

Create from a foundation of wholeness, not hustle.
Let your inner alignment do the heavy lifting.

This Week's Message

Prosperity and health don't arise from hustle. They flow when you create space for them.

One of the most powerful lessons I've learned is from the **Vacuum Law of Prosperity**.

You must let go of the old before you can receive the new.

Sometimes, what we need to release isn't just clutter. It's old beliefs, habits, or versions of ourselves that no longer serve our highest good.

At the end of every year, my husband and I sit down with a glass of wine to reflect on our goals. We laugh, we review, and we celebrate. And every year, we notice the same thing: the more we let go, the more room we create for health, joy, and abundance.

Letting go isn't always easy. But here's one practice that helped me train my mind (and my energy) to detach with grace: start simple.

- ★ Clean your garage. Donate what no longer serves you.
- ★ Clear out your closet, even just one drawer.
- ★ Delete apps, emails, or digital clutter you're no longer using.

Each act of letting go is a signal to Infinite Intelligence. *I'm ready for something new.* Your external environment reflects your internal alignment. Clearing space around you shifts the vibration within you.

You don't need to force your goals into being. Just **clear the space**, hold the vision, and trust that what's yours is already on the way.

Pause & Reflect

What beliefs or habits am I still holding on to that may be blocking prosperity or well-being?

_____
_____
_____
_____
_____
_____
_____
_____
_____
_____
_____

What would it feel like to create more spaciousness in my mind, body, or home?

_____
_____
_____
_____
_____
_____
_____
_____
_____

Pause & Reflect

Where in my life am I trying to control instead of allowing?

_____
_____
_____
_____
_____
_____
_____
_____
_____
_____

What physical space could I clear this week to practice the Vacuum Law of Prosperity?

_____
_____
_____
_____
_____
_____
_____
_____
_____

Pause & Reflect

What does prosperity mean to me, beyond just money?

_____
_____
_____
_____
_____
_____
_____
_____
_____
_____

How can I let go with more ease, knowing something better is ready to arrive?

_____
_____
_____
_____
_____
_____
_____
_____
_____

Anchor This Truth

"I am open, clear, and ready. I release what no longer serves me and welcome prosperity and health with ease."

Write your own version of this affirmation, or describe how it resonates with you today.

_____
_____
_____
_____
_____
_____
_____
_____
_____
_____
_____
_____
_____
_____
_____
_____
_____
_____
_____
_____
_____
_____
_____
_____
_____

Inner Voice Journal

Use this space to reflect on what came up during the message and the weekly questions.

You might write about:
- A space (physical or emotional) you cleared
- A belief or habit you're ready to let go of
- What prosperity and health feel like in your body

Let your Inner Voice speak freely.

Week 11: Be Confident, Even with an Empty Bank Account

True confidence isn't in the numbers; it's in your identity, vibration, and trust in the process.

This Week's Message

To stop being broke, you must begin with something most people overlook: **faith**.

I know what it feels like to open your account and see nothing. It's not just the numbers. It's the emotion that comes with it: fear, pressure, even shame.

But here's the truth that changed everything for me: your financial reality is a reflection of your **mindset**, not a life sentence.

One day, I decided: *I'm not available for this anymore.* And slowly, consistently, money started flowing to me with more ease.

Here are three steps that helped me shift from fear to flow.

Be Grateful for What You Already Have

You attract what you *feel*, not what you want. If you're stuck in frustration, you'll attract more reasons to feel frustrated. But when you feel true gratitude — even for something as simple as clean water, a roof, or a smile — you raise your vibration and open the door to more.

Learn Something New

During my lowest financial moments, I turned to personal development books. I knew my mind had to change before my reality could. Learning reminds you that you are capable, creative, and full of possibilities.

Make a Soulful Plan

Everything is happening *for* you, even the challenges. Ask, "What can I learn from this moment? What new skill or connection can help me move forward?"

Write your financial goal on paper.

"I am so happy and grateful now that I have $____."

**Read it. Believe it. Feel it.
Imagine it as already true.**

_____
_____
_____
_____
_____
_____
_____
_____
_____
_____

Confidence doesn't come from the number in your bank account. It comes from your vibration, identity, and trust in the process. Claim who you are becoming right now.

Pause & Reflect

How do I usually feel when I think about money?

_____
_____
_____
_____
_____
_____
_____
_____
_____
_____

What am I truly grateful for in my life right now?

_____
_____
_____
_____
_____
_____
_____
_____
_____
_____

Pause & Reflect

What beliefs or habits around money am I ready to shift?

_____
_____
_____
_____
_____
_____
_____
_____
_____
_____

What's one thing I could learn this week to support my financial growth?

_____
_____
_____
_____
_____
_____
_____
_____
_____
_____

Pause & Reflect

What's one aligned action I could take to open new opportunities?

_____
_____
_____
_____
_____
_____
_____
_____
_____
_____

How can I show up *today* as someone who already feels confident and abundant?

_____
_____
_____
_____
_____
_____
_____
_____

Anchor This Truth

"I am confident, abundant, and magnetic, no matter the numbers. My energy creates my reality."

Write your own version of this affirmation, or reflect on what it means to you.

_____
_____
_____
_____
_____
_____
_____
_____
_____
_____
_____
_____
_____
_____
_____
_____
_____
_____
_____
_____
_____
_____
_____
_____

Inner Voice Journal

Use this space to reflect on your emotions, breakthroughs, or shifts related to confidence and money.

You might explore:
- A financial fear you're ready to release
- A moment of confidence you reclaimed
- How you felt when you declared your financial goal on paper

Let your Inner Voice speak freely.

Week 12: Be the Source of Abundance

*Abundance flows to those who live it from within.
Radiate, give, and become magnetic.*

This Week's Message

In *The Science of Getting Rich*, Wallace Wattles teaches a powerful principle: "Leave everyone with the impression of increase."

Why? Because abundance is not just something we receive. It's something we embody and radiate.

All living things are wired for increase. It's the nature of life to expand, to grow, to reach for more — more beauty, more connection, more joy, more meaning. When we embrace this truth, we stop seeing desire as selfish and start seeing it as sacred.

And when we *live* from that space — when we are generous with our energy, our words, our presence — we become a source of abundance. Not just for ourselves but for everyone we meet.

Here are simple ways to live this truth each day:

- ★ Give sincere compliments.
- ★ Smile, and use people's names.
- ★ Point out others' strengths and wins.
- ★ Ask real questions, and listen with full presence.
- ★ Acknowledge the small things others do.

At first, it might feel unnatural. But the more you give, the more you feel your own abundance. The more you lift others, the more you rise.

You are already abundant. Let your life reflect it. Be the increase.

Pause & Reflect

What does abundance mean to me, beyond material things?

_____
_____
_____
_____
_____
_____
_____
_____
_____
_____

In what areas of my life do I already feel abundant?

_____
_____
_____
_____
_____
_____
_____
_____
_____
_____

Pause & Reflect

How can I leave others with the impression of increase this week?

_____
_____
_____
_____
_____
_____
_____
_____
_____
_____

What's one simple act I can do today to lift someone else?

_____
_____
_____
_____
_____
_____
_____
_____

Pause & Reflect

What blocks me from feeling or sharing abundance, and how can I release it?

_____
_____
_____
_____
_____
_____
_____
_____
_____
_____
_____

What will change if I see myself as a source of abundance everywhere I go?

_____
_____
_____
_____
_____
_____
_____
_____
_____

Anchor This Truth

**"I am abundance in action.
I give freely, receive joyfully, and uplift everyone around me."**

Write your own version of this affirmation, or reflect on how it feels in your heart and body.

_____
_____
_____
_____
_____
_____
_____
_____
_____
_____
_____
_____
_____
_____
_____
_____
_____
_____
_____
_____
_____
_____
_____

Inner Voice Journal

Use this final journaling space to explore your relationship with abundance — not just what you want to attract but how you're already living it.

You might reflect on:
- A moment this week when you gave without expecting
- A time you lifted someone and felt filled yourself
- How you see yourself differently now, at the end of this journey

Let your Inner Voice speak freely.

Closing Reflection: You Did It

Twelve weeks ago, you made a decision — to come home to yourself.

You didn't just journal.
You showed up.
You reflected.
You softened.
You listened.

And whether it felt powerful or subtle, something has shifted.

You've explored your mindset.
You've practiced new habits.
You've chosen faith, clarity, and trust.

And maybe, for the first time in a long time, you've remembered …

You are powerful.
You are wise.
You are magnetic.

This journal was never about becoming someone else. It was always about **becoming more of who you already are** — whole, abundant, worthy, and deeply connected to your Inner Voice.

Take a moment now to honor that.

Final Reflection Questions

What have I discovered about myself over the past twelve weeks?

_____
_____
_____
_____
_____
_____
_____
_____
_____
_____

What inner shifts am I most proud of?

_____
_____
_____
_____
_____
_____
_____
_____
_____

Final Reflection Questions

Which weekly lesson had the biggest impact on me and why?

_____
_____
_____
_____
_____
_____
_____
_____
_____
_____

What do I now believe about myself that I didn't fully believe before?

_____
_____
_____
_____
_____
_____
_____
_____
_____

Final Reflection Questions

How will I continue to nurture this version of me — the one who is aligned, peaceful, and ready for more?

_____
_____
_____
_____
_____
_____
_____
_____
_____
_____
_____

What evidence do I have that I'm not the same person I was when I began this journal?

_____
_____
_____
_____
_____
_____
_____
_____

Closing Affirmation

*"I trust myself. I am aligned with my truth.
I welcome what's next with joy and ease."*

Write a message to your future self. What do you want her to remember? What has she already accomplished? What do you want her to *feel*?

Dear Future Me ...

A Note from Ana

Thank you for walking this journey with me.

You made a powerful choice by showing up for yourself — not just once but again and again, even when life felt messy or uncertain.

If it took you longer than twelve weeks to complete this journal, please don't be discouraged. This isn't about being perfect. It's about choosing presence. And each time you paused to reflect, breathe, and listen to your Inner Voice, you shifted something meaningful within.

This journal isn't meant to be a one-time experience. The decision to live with clarity, confidence, and peace is a **daily practice**. Each round of this journey reveals new layers because *you're growing*.

I created this journal to help you make small but powerful mental shifts so that you can start seeing your life through a new lens — one of possibility, alignment, and self-trust. The more you use this tool, the more transformation you'll see.

When you're ready, I encourage you to begin again with a new journal. Go through the weekly lessons once more, and compare your answers. Notice how your thinking has evolved. Celebrate how far you've come.

"We don't improve what we don't track."

You are not behind. You are not failing. You are transforming — beautifully, steadily, in your own divine timing.

I'm cheering you on, always.

With love and gratitude,

Ana

I'd Love to Hear from You!

Thank you for choosing the *The Graceful Healing Workbook & Journal*, a tool I created with deep intention to help others practice the principles that create real transformation from the inside out.

Starting a new habit, especially one that asks us to slow down and reflect, isn't always easy. That's why I designed this journal to feel both grounded and inspiring. Week by week, it guides you to reconnect with your inner voice, align with your desires, and take gentle action toward the life you truly want to live.

This journal is more than just prompts and pages. It's a companion, a space where you get to explore your beliefs, shift your energy, and become a conscious creator of your reality.

If this journal has supported you in any way, I would be so grateful if you'd take a moment to leave a review. Your feedback helps others discover if *The Graceful Healing Workbook & Journal* is right for them, and it helps me continue creating meaningful tools for your growth.

You can leave a review on Amazon or Goodreads, or share your story on social media and tag me. I read every message and every review. Your words matter deeply to me.

Thank you for being part of this growing community of conscious manifestors.

With love,

Ana

Your Journey Doesn't End Here

Congratulations on completing this chapter of your *The Graceful Healing Workbook & Journal* journey! By showing up each week, reflecting, and taking small aligned steps, you've done something powerful. You've invested in your inner world.

But this is just the beginning.

Imagine where you could be a few months from now — with deeper clarity, stronger mental habits, and a life that flows from peace, not pressure. That's the kind of life you're creating, one week at a time. If you're ready to keep growing and want more structured guidance, my *Gratitude Life Design* program expands on the principles in this journal. It offers deeper tools and lessons to help you build a life of resilience, purpose, and joy.

In this online program, you'll learn how to:

- **Transform limiting beliefs**: Discover why it's challenging to build new habits, and uncover the paradigms holding you back from your fullest potential.

- **Anchor daily gratitude rituals**: Create simple, meaningful practices that make gratitude an effortless part of every day.

- **Build emotional resilience**: Use gratitude to face life's challenges with strength and stability, experiencing greater peace in the process.

- **Manifest abundance**: Combine gratitude with powerful visualization techniques to attract health, joy, prosperity, and fulfilling relationships.

- **Deepen self-love**: Grow in compassion toward yourself, and align your actions with your highest values and goals.

If you're ready to design a life that reflects your deepest desires, I invite you to join me on this transformative journey. *Gratitude Life Design* will support you every step of the way, helping you create a life you truly love.

GratitudeLifeDesign.com

Keep going. You have the power to design a beautiful, gratitude-centered life. I'm so excited to be a part of your journey!

Additional Resources to Support Your Journey

Thank you for walking this path with me. If you're feeling inspired to continue your growth and want more guidance as you deepen your mental habits and inner connection, I've created a few resources just for you.

Read *I Trust My Inner Voice*

Discover more about how to connect with your Inner Voice and make decisions that resonate with your true self. Get your copy today on Amazon.

Join My Reader Group: *Manifest Mondays*

Dive deeper into the journey of self-discovery and personal growth with my weekly email newsletter, *Manifest Mondays*. As a member of my reader group, you'll receive exclusive insights, tips, and stories directly from me, helping you manifest your desires and live your best life. Each Monday, I explore new themes that inspire, motivate, and empower you to take actionable steps toward achieving your dreams.

Benefits of Joining:

- **Inspiration Delivered Weekly:** Kickstart every week with a fresh perspective. *Manifest Mondays* offers motivational insights and practical advice to help you navigate the challenges of daily life while striving toward your highest aspirations.

- **Empowerment for Your Personal Journey:** Each email is crafted to empower you with the tools and confidence to apply manifestation principles to your personal and professional life, ensuring continuous growth and achievement.

It's more than a newsletter. It's a weekly ritual of reflection, support, and alignment.

Join here:

anaparravivas.com/weekly-inspirational-emails

Or scan the QR code below to sign up instantly.

Social Networks

Connect with me, and join our online community for daily inspiration and practical advice.

🅾 @ana_parra_vivas

🅕 fb.com/anaparravivas

I hope to continue being part of your path to a fuller and more conscious life. See you soon!

I TRUST MY INNER VOICE

"If you are tired of feeling stuck in life, you must read *I Trust My Inner Voice*! You will find easy, applicable tools you can use to transform your own thoughts and create a life you love. I love Ana's authenticity in her writing. She is easy to relate to, and I am excited to see all the good things that I am manifesting, thanks to this book."

— Wendy Cardell, mother, wife, entrepreneur

About the Author

Ana Parra Vivas believes that each of us can achieve great things when we understand our capabilities. Ana grew up in a difficult environment, and from a young age, she did not believe in herself. When she was eighteen, she changed her perspective when she learned about success through the book *Manual del Exito* by Camilo F. Cruz, Ph.D. (English title: *Success Manual*). Ana became determined to improve her life.

After achieving what she wanted in her career and family life, Ana found herself in a hole once more. She felt frustrated and guilty that her career was taking away time with her children, and she did not feel fulfilled as a woman. All of these negative feelings and thoughts caused her stress and anxiety. As a result, her health started to break down, and everything she had built, including her family, started to fall like a house of cards. She decided to study herself, and ultimately, she discovered the tools that brought her balance as she recovered her personal power.

Today, Ana is a multi-award-winning author of self-development books and journals, including *I Trust My Inner Voice* and *Quantum Gratitude*. Her work helps readers slow down, listen within, and take small, aligned actions toward a more peaceful, powerful life.

With a voice that is both simple and deeply moving, Ana writes for women who are ready to stop striving and start creating from a place of truth. Her tools don't just inspire; they transform.

To explore Ana's books and resources, visit www.AnaParraVivas.com

www.ingramcontent.com/pod-product-compliance
Lightning Source LLC
LaVergne TN
LVHW081545070526
838199LV00057B/3782